GROWING THOUGHTS

LAZY SQUID

Dedicating this book to all the hearts filled with love.

Contents

Foreword

I will not write that the write-ups are my imagination because it makes the story real. I just want to say- don't read my book just feel it.

Preface

This Book is all about feelings of hearts whether your love is one-sided or you are heart broken, doesn't matter if you are in love, this book includes all types of heart.

1. The Sweetest Gift

Enter Caption

Thanks love for the sweetest gift,

You returned with the biggest rift.

After so many months and years,

We met and celebrated with beers.

I saw, Flashing call on your phone,

Number was saved with “my own”.

I just ignored believing blindly in you,

You were looking gorgeous in blue.

One day you called me to meet soon,

I became very happy thinking it boon.

But where my smile had gone when,

You decided to break up. After then,

You went and blocked my number,

I tried to contact you but you were

gone already too much far from me.

Thanks love, for gifting this to me.

2. Love Game

Enter Caption

Downloaded me in his

eyes at first sight.

Logged in my life by

facebook friend request.

Uploaded ammunition in the

form of loving words.

Loading process ended in

two or three months.

Then started playing,

continuosly played for

almost three years.

Yuck! this is so boring. He

thought to try something new.

And selected this Old

"Love Game" app and

deleted. Now he has downloaded

new game app in his life

and started playing.

Chapter3

Enter Caption

He stopped her when

she talked to another boys.

Told her it is not good

to talk to every boy.

Now she doesn't talk to

others. He thought that

she is impressed by him.

Both started talking to each

other . One day she told him

I wanna click a pic with you.

He was really very happy that

day. He agreed in one breath.

She clicked many pics. Now they

went to their own home. He was

too excited. Waiting eagerly for

next day for seeing her.

wow! what a beautiful love story.

Hold on! Hold on! There is more

to say about their love.

one of his friends told him

that she uploaded his pictures

on WhatsApp. He became very happy

and told him to show. Ah! pictures

were awesome with great caption like

my hero, hotty and so on. Don't

ask about his heartbeat because

that was more than abnormal.

we all are celebrating that

happiness and then ....

And then last pic in status,

which took smile of him

along with us in the air. The

caption-which made him heart broken,

the caption-which made her heart breaker

that was "my brother, you are

a real super hero for me."

4. Love and its manifestation

Enter Caption

If missing you is madness

and this madness is love

then i want to be mad forever.

If texting you repeatedly is loss of self-respect

and this loss of self-respect is love

then I want to lose self-respect everytime.

If waking up for you till morning is foolishness

and this foolishness is love

then i want to be fool till my last breath.

If waiting for you is waste of time

and this waste of time is love

then i want to waste my time whole life.

If thinking of you is obsession

and being obsessed is love

then i want to be obsessed for always.

If writing about you is my passion

and this passion is love

then I want to be passionate for lifetime.

If loving you is weakness

and this weakness is love

then i want to be weak more and more

5. One-hearted Love

Enter Caption

To love someone

With full devotion

It happens in

One-sided love only.

To smell someone's presence

before that one's appearance

It happens in

One-sided love only.

To live with someone

Without being quarrelsome

It happens in

One-sided love only.

To love someone

Without telling that one

It happens in

One-sided love only.

6. And suddenly he left me

Enter Caption

Left me! Really he left me.

don't know when and why?

But it's true he left me.

No any fight, no argument

Don't know why but he left me.

In the dusk we are together,

he was holding me in his arms

and we were watching sunset.

Everything was really fine.But

without telling me he left me.

Yeah , yeah I remembered

his phone was flashing

I asked but he changed

the topic with loving words.

He used to say he loves me.

He loves me but he left me.

I don't the reason but without

saying goodbye he left me.

yeah, you heard right he left me.

7. A letter to love

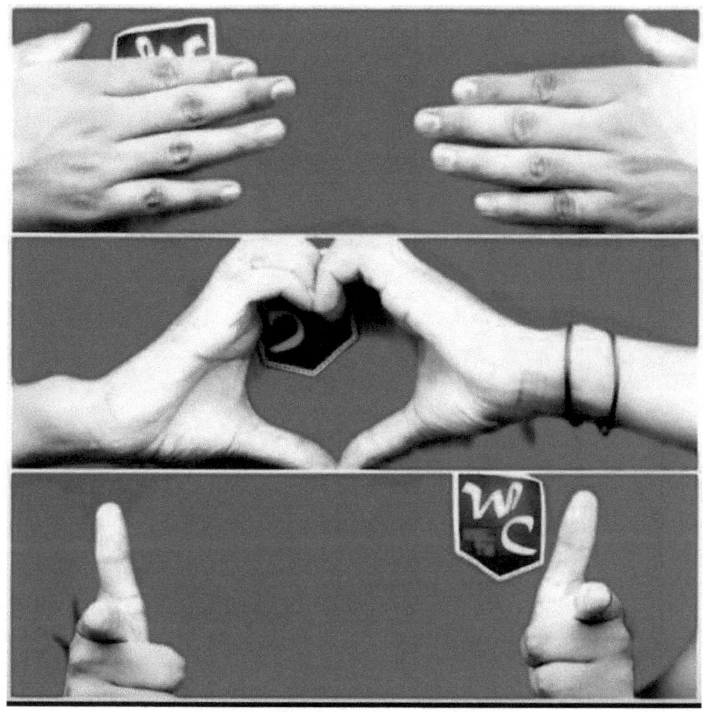

Enter Caption

Dear ,

How are you? I'm fine here. You too must be fine. Have you forgotten me or don't want to remember? You know I am missing you in my every breath. I was just scrolling down photos. I found a picture of ours which made my fingers numb. The picture which reminds me of you , which reminds me that you are present in my heart and in my mind. We had to go to new coaching for your entrance exam preparation. But we didn't go and went to the theatre. We enjoyed a lot and came home. Next morning, I bunked my class and we went on the long morning walk. Dear , do you remember or not? You clicked pictures and made video of our shadows without telling me. After few days you sent me all those pictures and the special shadow video of ours when I fought with you.

You are so smart.You knew that I'll forget fight after seeing our photos. You knew all the formulae of making me happy. Then what happened now? What's wrong with you? Why don't you understand my feelings even after telling so many times? Why dear, tell me why? I really want to know. If you have any problem, tell me. If you have any problem with me, then also tell me. But please don't leave me. It's really tough to live without you. I am sending this letter to you. It's up to you to reply or not. But i'll keep writing letters to you. I can stop only when i'll get answer from your side. Dear remember this,I am not going to stop thinking about you and loving you.

I'm waiting for your reply eagerly. You know i go to the door so fast even when postman comes with the pan card delivery or for papa's courier in the hope of getting your letter, in the hope of getting your reply. I wish you miss me a lot. Take care of your family and yourself. And yeah don't forget to miss me. Lots of love for you.

Only yours

8. Lovebirds Chat

Enter Caption

He— Hi dear.

I— Oh! You got time to message me. Say.

He— I have always time for you, my dear.

I— I know, I know, no need to explain me.

He— Please don't quarrel. You never talk to me with love.

I— I use to be in fighting mood! Wow great then don't talk to me. Bye.

He— Please don't say bye. I want to talk to you.

I— But I don't.

He— Sure!

I— say, what do you want to say?

He— Today you say something.

I—- you know I have done a mistake not small but a big mistake.

He —— What ?

I —- I loved .

He —- So .

I —— I loved not a normal person but an antique piece.

He —- Love you.

(Twist in conversation)

I —- But now I want to correct my mistake.

He —- what do you want to say??? Say clearly. I'm your mistake and you want to leave me!

(He becomes angry and very sad).

I— No you are my love and in love there is no place for mistake but love. Love you.

He— Then what about mistake?

I—- Nothing, I was just teasing you.

He —- Don't change topic. (With smile) By the way love you too.

I— Bye. My class is going to start. Talk to you after class.

He— Okay bye. I'm waiting for your message. Love you too much.

I— Love you too. Love you so much. Bye. Take care.

9. Loving hate

Enter Caption

Oh love! I hate you.

You made me intoxicated

by seeing in my eyes.

And then you closed

Your eyes by my side!

That's not fair . That's why

Oh love! I hate you.

You became my hand

by helping me always

whenever I need help.

And now you showed

thumb and went away!

That's not fair. That's why

Oh love! I hate you.

Oh my love! I love you too

for loving me, for being

with me always. I love

you for being fan in summer

and for being heater in winter.

Maybe for sometime but you

Came, that's enough for me.

That's really enough. That's why

Oh love! I still love you.

10. Smelly love

Enter Caption

You smell like toffee

which is my smile key.

You smell like wine,

for you,makes me pine

You smell like pickle.

makes my tongue fickle.

You smell like tea

creates scenario of sea.

You smell like food

makes me selfish and rude.

You smell like morning

makes me feel you are calling.

You smell like day

gives me hope of ray.

You smell like night

gives the paradise sight.

You smell like dream

gives me happiness beam.

Oh love! You smell like spring

makes me to write and sing.

11. Arrival of the second coming

Enter Caption

Perhaps that Spiritus Mundi is born,

Coming towards the world from Bethlehem.

Those fatty thighs moving fast to us.

Not in the shape of half animal -half human body,

But in the form of immorality appearance.

Ah! I know it doesn't tremble our hearts.

Even nightmares do not make us awake.

because we think ourselves as superior one.

Unaware of that our envy, hatred became our superiors.

These Immoralities started ruling our hearts and thoughts.

Became the weapon for killing one another.

One day we will die with the weapon prepared by ourselves.

That day this world will become hatred and Jealousy free.

Only that day world will take a relief breath.

9 798886 297799

Printed by Libri Plureos GmbH in Hamburg, Germany